ISBN 978-1-334-70019-4
PIBN 10625068

1 MONTH OF
FREE
READING

at

www.ForgottenBooks.com

By purchasing this book you are eligible for one month membership to ForgottenBooks.com, giving you unlimited access to our entire collection of over 700,000 titles via our web site and mobile apps.

To claim your free month visit:

www.forgottenbooks.com/free625068

English
Français
Deutsche
Italiano
Español
Português

www.forgottenbooks.com

Mythology Photography **Fiction**
Fishing Christianity **Art** Cooking
Essays Buddhism Freemasonry
Medicine **Biology** Music **Ancient
Egypt** Evolution Carpentry Physics
Dance Geology **Mathematics** Fitness
Shakespeare **Folklore** Yoga Marketing
Confidence Immortality Biographies
Poetry **Psychology** Witchcraft
Electronics Chemistry History **Law**
Accounting **Philosophy** Anthropology
Alchemy Drama Quantum Mechanics
Atheism Sexual Health **Ancient History**
Entrepreneurship Languages Sport
Paleontology Needlework Islam
Metaphysics Investment Archaeology
Parenting Statistics Criminology
Motivational

SONNETS
FROM THE PORTUGUESE

BY ELIZABETH BARRETT BROWNING

Portland, Maine
THOMAS B. MOSHER

INTRODUCTION

THE SONNETS FROM THE PORTUGUESE.

IT was in the second or 1850 edition of the *Poems in two volumes* that the *Sonnets from the Portuguese* were first given to the public. The circumstances attending their composition have never been clearly related. Mr. Browning, however, eight years before his death, made a statement to a friend, with the understanding that at some future date, after his own decease, the story might be more widely told. The time seems to have arrived when there can be no possible indiscretion in recording a very pretty episode of literary history.

During the months of their brief courtship, closing, as all the world knows, in the clandestine flight and romantic wedding of September 12, 1846, neither poet showed any verses to the other. Mr. Browning, in particular, had not the smallest notion that

the circumstances of their betrothal had led
Miss Barrett into any artistic expression of
feeling. As little did he suspect it during
their honeymoon in Paris, or during their
first crowded weeks in Italy. They settled,
at length, in Pisa; and being quitted by Mrs.
Jamieson and her niece, in a very calm and
happy mood the young couple took up each
his or her separate literary work.

Their custom was, Mr. Browning said,
to write alone, and not to show each other
what they had written. This was a rule
which he sometimes broke through, but she
never. He had the habit of working in a
downstairs room, where their meals were
spread, while Mrs. Browning studied in a
room on the floor above. One day, early in
1847, their breakfast being over, Mrs. Brown-
ing went upstairs, while her husband stood
at the window watching the street till the
table should be cleared. He was presently
aware of some one behind him, although the
servant was gone. It was Mrs. Browning,
who held him by the shoulder to prevent his
turning to look at her, and at the same time
pushed a packet of papers into the pocket
of his coat. She told him to read that, and
to tear it up if he did not like it; and then
she fled again to her own room.

Mr. Browning seated himself at the table,

and unfolded the parcel. It contained the series of sonnets which have now become so illustrious. As he read, his emotion and delight may be conceived. Before he had finished it was impossible for him to restrain himself, and, regardless of his promise, he rushed upstairs, and stormed that guarded citadel. He was early conscious that these were treasures not to be kept from the world; " I dared not reserve to myself," he said, " the finest sonnets written in any language since Shakespeare's." But Mrs. Browning was very loth indeed to consent to the publication of what had been the very notes and chronicle of her betrothal. At length she was persuaded to permit her friend, Miss Mary Russell Mitford, to whom they had originally been sent in manuscript, to pass them through the press, although she absolutely declined to accede to Miss Mitford's suggestion that they should appear in one of the fashionable annuals of the day. Accordingly a small volume was printed entitled *Sonnets* | *by* | *E. B. B.* | *Reading* | *Not for Publication* | 1847 | , an octavo of 47 pages.

When it was determined to publish the sonnets in the volumes of 1850, the question of a title arose. The name which was ultimately chosen, *Sonnets from the Portuguese,* was invented by Mr. Browning, as an ingenious device to veil the true authorship, and yet to suggest kinship with that beautiful lyric, called *Catarina to Camoens*, in which so similar a passion had been expressed. Long before he ever heard of these poems, Mr. Browning called his wife his "own little Portuguese," and so, when she proposed "Sonnets translated from the Bosnian," he, catching at the happy thought of "translated," replied, "No, not Bosnian—that means nothing—but from the Portuguese! They are Catarina's sonnets!" And so, in half a joke, half a conceit, the famous title was invented.

I

The psychological moment at which the *Sonnets from the Portuguese* were composed, was one of singular importance. Although she was in her forty-first year (according to some accounts, in her thirty-eighth), the genius of Elizabeth Barrett was but newly come to its maturity. In precocity of intelligence she had been so remarkable as to become a type of childish attainment, but as an artist she was very slow to develop. Her earliest writings were strictly imitative; the volumes she published in her young womanhood were full of interesting passages, but

crude and jejune to an extraordinary degree.
Had Elizabeth Barrett died at the age of
thirty-three,* that is to say immediately after
the publication of *The Seraphim*, she would
scarcely live among the English poets. It
is to a subsequent period, it is to the years
between the loss of her brother Edward at
Torquay and her marriage, that those poems
belong which display her talent at their
highest achievement. The two volumes of
1844 lifted her by a bound to the highest
place among the living poets of her country,
and seated her by the side of Tennyson.
These two, in the genial old age of Words-
worth, were left the sole obvious inheritors
of his throne, for Robert Browning was still
obscure save to a very few.

The change that in those years preceding
her betrothal had come to Elizabeth Barrett
was a purifying and crystallising one. She
had always had fire, and she was to keep the
coal burning on her tongue, like the prophet,
until the end of her career. But in the early
period, and again in the period of her decline,
what was lacking was light. Her style was
turbid ; the poet was not Sappho, standing
in sunlight on the cliff of Mitylene, but

---

* I take for granted that the Coxhoe date of her
birth, March 6, 1806, must be the correct one. But the
crux seems still unsettled.

Pythia, seated in the smoke and vapour of Delphi, tortured by the vehemence of her own utterance, torn by the message which she lacked the art to deliver. Critics are beginning to see now, and sorrowfully to admit, that what is causing the noble figure of Elizabeth Barrett to recede gradually from that front place in which Tennyson, for instance, and Keats hold their pre-eminence, is her turbidity. The best poetry may roll down violent places, but it remains as limpid as a trout-stream; what is unfortunate about Mrs. Browning's is that it is constantly stained and clouded.

But there was a period—we may roughly date it between 1842 and 1850—when these radical faults affected her style least. It was then that she reached the zenith of her genius, and, by a strange and fortunate accident, it was then, also, that she attained her greatest sum of happiness and health. Of this highest period, the summit or peak was the short space during which Robert Browning visited her as her affianced lover, and it is not singular, perhaps, but it is at least very interesting and pleasing, to find her writings at that moment less affected than at any other time, before or afterwards, by the errors which beset her.

In other words, the *Sonnets from the*

Portuguese, although they are by no means of equal merit, reach at their best the highest art of which their author was capable, and if we did not possess them, we should be forced to form a considerably lower estimate of her possibilities as an artist than we now do. She seems in the very best of her work, outside the volumes of 1844, to be utterly indifferent to technical excellence. Even in those volumes we see that her laxity was absolutely inherent, and that she is always liable to imperfection and licence. But the *Sonnets from the Portuguese* prove that she could, at her purest, throw off these stains and blemishes, and cast her work in bronze, like a master. They show her to us at her very best, and they form the pinnacle of her edifice as an artistic constructor. Perhaps, and to some readers, they may be neither the most attractive nor the most amusing of her writings, but to the critic they are certainly the least imperfect.

II

The natural bent of Elizabeth Barrett was certainly not to the sonnet. She was too dithyrambic, too tumultuous, to be willingly restrained within a rigid form of verse. She employed none other of the regular English metres, except blank verse, which she treated with a sort of defiant desperation, and *terza rima,* in which she successfully strangled her genius. Her lyrics are all of her own invention or adaptation, and they are commonly of a loose, wild form, fit to receive her chains of adverbial caprices and her tempestuous assonances. But her love of Shakespeare and Wordsworth drove her to emulation, and once and again she strove to bind her ebullient melodies down to the strict mould of fourteen rhymed iambics. It is evident that the difficulties she encountered piqued her to return to the attack, for her occasional sonnets became moie and more frequent. It is interesting to note that, as befitted so learned a student of the Italians, her sonnets, from the first, were accurately built on the Petrarchan model. We might have expected from her usual laxity of form an adherence to the Elizabethan quatorzain, or, at least, to some of those adaptations in which Wordsworth, Coleridge, and even Keats indulged. But Miss Barrett, throughout her career, was one of the most rigid of Petrarchans, and no fault can be found with the structure of her octetts and sestetts.

One of the earliest sonnets of her mature period was that entitled " The Soul's Expression," which is so interesting as a revelation of her own consciousness of the difficulties which technical art presented to her, and so valuable an indication of the mode in which she approached the sonnet-form, that it may here be quoted : —

With stammering lips and insufficient sound,
I strive and struggle to deliver right
That music of my nature, day and night
With dream and thought and feeling, inter-
*   wound,*
And inly answering all the senses round
With octaves of a mystic depth and height,
Which step out grandly to the infinite
From the dark edges of the sensual ground!
This song of soul I struggle to outbear
Through portals of the sense, sublime and
*   whole,*
And utter all myself into the air :
But if I did it—as the thunder-roll
Breaks its own cloud—my flesh would perish
*   there,*
Before that dread apocalypse of soul.

Fine as this is, eminently true to her own mood, and singular for its self-knowledge, it cannot be said to promise for its writer any great felicity as a sonneteer. The perturbed imagery, the wild grammar, the lack of a clarified and disciplined conception of style are prominent in every line. Very much more

9

successful, however, and plainly inspired by the study of Wordsworth, is the famous sonnet, "On a Portrait by R. B. Haydon," and in the years that immediately followed her return from Torquay, Miss Barrett's sonnets came thicker and faster, with a steady increase in the power to give her own peculiar characteristics of expression to this unfamiliar instrument. But the *Sonnets from the Portuguese* went further still. The little harp or lyre she had laboriously taught herself to perform upon, had just become familiar to her fingers, when it was called upon to record emotions the most keen, and imaginations the most subtle, which had ever crossed the creative brain of its possessor.

Great technical beauty, therefore, is the mark of these wonderful poems. Not merely are the rhymes arranged with a rare science and with a precision which few other English poets have had the patience to preserve, but the tiresome faults of Miss Barrett's prosody, those little foxes which habitually spoil her grapes, are here marvellously absent. Her very ear, which sometimes seemed so dull, with its "morning" and "inurning," its "Bacchantes" and "grant us," here seems to be quickened and strung into acuteness. There is a marked absence, in the *Sonnets from the Portuguese,* of all slovenly false rhymes, of all careless half-meaningless locutions, of all practical jokes played upon the parts of speech. The cycle opens with a noble dignity, and it is, on the whole, preserved at that high ethical level of distinguished poetic utterance.

Of sonnet-cycles in the English language, there are but very few which can even be mentioned in connection with that which we are describing. In the Elizabethan age, many crowns woven of fourteen-petalled blossoms were laid at the feet of unknown ladies. The art which invested these groups of sonnets was mainly of a thin and conventional order. It would task the memory or the instinct of the best of English scholars to tell at sight whether a given sonnet came from the garland of *Idea* or of *Fidessa,* of *Delia* or of *Chloris.* Two cycles in that age immensely surpassed all the rest, and we may safely say that the *Amoretti* of Spenser form a set of poems as much greater than those we have mentioned, as they are inferior to Shakespeare's. In later times, we have one or two deliberate sets of sonnets by Wordsworth, and since the days of Mrs. Browning, Rossetti's *House of Life.* In foreign poetry, it is natural to turn to the *Sonettenkranz,* in which, in 1807, Goethe darkly celebrated his passion for Minna Herzlieb, the mysterious Ottilie of the *Wahlverwandtschaften*. Among the five best or most striking prolonged poems in the sonnet-form which English literature possesses, Miss Barrett's, however, must unquestionably be reckoned. No competent critic could put the languid sweetness and honeyed vagueness of Spenser's daisy-chain of quatorzains in a rank so high as these serried, nervous, and highly-developed poems must hold, while Wordsworth, perfect as he constantly is in the evolution of a single sonnet, is scarcely to be applauded for his conduct of any such series of such poems, nor *The River Duddon* or *The Ecclesiastical Sonnets* to be compared for vital interest with those we are considering. Miss Barrett, accordingly, is left, on this occasion, with but two competitors. Rossetti excels her by the volume and impetus of his imagery, and by his voluptuous intrepidity, but she holds her own by the intense vivacity of her instinct and the sincerity of her picture of emotion. Beside the immortal melodies of Shakespeare, hers may be counted voluble, harsh, and slight; but even here, her sympathy with a universal passion, the freshness and poignancy with which she treats a mood that is not rare and almost sickly, not foreign to the common experience of mankind, but eminently normal, direct, and obvious, give her a curious advantage. It is probable that the sonnets written by Shakespeare to his friend contain lovelier poetry and a style more perennially admirable, but those addressed by Elizabeth Barrett to her lover are hardly less exquisite to any of us, and to many of us are more wholesome and more intelligible.

III

Sincerity, indeed, is the first gift in literature, and perhaps the most uncommon. It is not granted to more than a few to express in precise and direct language their most powerful emotional experiences. To those who, like Mary Magdalene, have loved much, the art is rarely given to define and differentiate their feelings. The attempt to render passion by artistic speech is commonly void of success to a pathetic degree. Those who have desired, enjoyed, and suffered to the very edge of human capacity, put the musical instrument to their lips to try and tell us what they felt, and the result is all discord and falsetto. There is no question that many of the coldest and most affected verses, such as we are apt to scorn for their tasteless weakness, must hide underneath the white ash of their linguistic poverty a core of red hot passion. But the rare art of literary sincerity has not been granted to these inarticulate lovers, and what cost them so many tears affords us nothing but fatigue or ridicule.

It is peculiarly true that women who are poets can or will but seldom take us truly into their confidence in this matter. A natural but unfortunate delicacy leads them to write of love so platonically or so obscurely that we cannot tell what it is they wish to communicate. Not to seem so unmaidenly as to address a man, they feign to be men themselves and languish at the ladies. We are as much interested and as much convinced as we are at the opera when broad-hipped cavaliers in silken tights dance with slightly shorter girls in skirts. It is a curious fact that the amount of love-poetry written by women, and openly addressed to men, is very scanty. Our poetesses write:

> *I made a posy for my Love*
> *As fair as she is soft and fine,*

and wonder that we are faintly interested. It should be "as tough as he is firm and strong," and then we might really be inclined to conclude that the ditty was inspired by experience or instinctive feeling. Lady

Winchelsea's honest praises of her husband, Ephelia's couplets on that false J. G. who sailed away to Tangier and never came back again, the sonnets of the fair rope-maker of Lyons, Louise Labé, the tender, thrilling lyrics written three hundred years later by Marceline Desbordes-Valmore — these are almost the only poems in all literature which one remembers as dealing, in lucidity and sincerity alike, with the love of a man by a woman.

But the keynote of Elizabeth Barrett as an artist was sincerity. It is this quality, with all that it implies, which holds together the edifice of her style, built of such incongruous materials that no less-tempered mortar could bind it into a compact whole. At no period of her literary life, even when she was too slavishly following obsolete or tasteless models, was she otherwise than sincere. She was not striving to produce an effect; she was trying with all the effort of which her spirit was capable, to say exactly what was in her heart. When sorrow possessed her, her verse sobbed and wailed with impatient human stress, and when at last, while she waited for Death to take her by the hair, it was Love instead who came, she poured forth the heart of a happy woman without stint or concealment. The typical instance of the former class is the poem called "De Profundis," written as soon after the drowning of her brother Edward as the shattered nerves and beaten brain permitted her to taste the solace of composition. It should be read, in spite of its comparative inferiority, in connection with the *Sonnets from the Portuguese*, for the power it reveals is the same; it is the capacity, while feeling acutely and deeply, to find appropriate, sufficient, and yet unexaggerated expression for the emotion. This great neuropathic artist was a physician as well as a sufferer, and could count her pulses accurately through all the spasms of her anguish and her ecstasy.

When, in 1866, Robert Browning published the first selection from his wife's poems, he arranged the pieces in such a way as to give unobtrusive emphasis to the connection between the *Sonnets from the Portuguese* and two short lyrics. Even if he had not placed "Question and Answer," and "Inclusions" immediately in front of the sonnet-cycle, we might have been justified in conjecturing that they belonged to the same period and the same mood. The arrangement of the *Sonnets* is historical. They are not heaped together in accidental sequence, as Spenser's and Shakespeare's seem to be, but they move

on from the first surprise of unexpected
passion to the final complete resignation of
soul and body in a rapture which is to be
sanctified and heightened by death itself.
It is therefore possible, I think, by careful
examination of the text, to insert in the
sequence of sonnets, at their obvious point
of composition, the two lyrics I have just
mentioned; and for that purpose I will
quote them here.

Taking the *Sonnets* in our hands, we meet
first with the record of the violent shock
produced on the whole being of the solitary
and fading recluse by the discovery that Love
—laughing Love masquerading under the
cowl of Death—has invaded her sequestered
chamber. Then to amazement succeeds
instinctive repulsion; she shrinks back in
a sort of horror, in her chilly twilight, from
the boisterous entrance of so much heat
and glow. But this quickly passes, also,
submerged in the sense of her own unworthi-
ness; her hands are numb, her eyes blinded
and dazed—what has this guest of kings to
do with her, a mourner in the dust? Then
follows, in a crescent movement of emotion,
the noble image of Electra, pouring her
sepulchral urn and all its ashes at the feet
of Love, ashes that blight and burn, an
affection so morbid and vain that it may

rather destroy than bless the heart which
provokes the gift   It is at this moment,
I think, between sonnets 5 and 6, that
"Question and Answer" should be read,
repeating the same idea, but repeating it in
a lower key, with less violence and perhaps
a shade less conviction:

Love you seek for, presupposes
    Summer heat and sunny glow.
Tell me, do you find moss-roses
    Budding, blooming in the snow ?
Snow might kill the rose-tree's root—
Shake it quickly from your foot,
    Lest it harm you as you go.

From the ivy where it dapples
    A grey ruin, stone by stone,
Do you look for grapes or apples,
    Or for sad green leaves alone ?
Pluck the leaves off, two or three—
Keep them for morality
    When you shall be safe and gone.

But above these flutterings of the capt-
ured heart the captor hangs enamoured and
persistent, smiling at the fiat which bids
him begone: and the heart begins to thaw

with the unrelieved radiation. The poetess acknowledges that she feels that she will stand henceforward in his shadow, that he has changed for her the face of all the world. Still, she dares not yield. The tide of her unworthiness flows up, and floods all the creeks of her being; she can but hide her eyes, from which the tears are flowing, and bid him, if he will not go and leave her, if he will persist in standing there with eloquent eyes fixed upon her, to trample on the pale stuff of her life, too dead to be taken to his arms. She is scarcely reasonable; we feel her pulses reeling, her limbs failing, and in the next sonnet the wave recedes for the final forward rush. She will not pour her poison on to his Venice-glass, she will not love him, will not see him—and in the next line she is folded to his arms, murmuring, " I love thee   I love thee ! "

From this point forward the sonnets play, in their exquisite masque, as if to celestial dance-music, with the wild thoughts and tremulous frolics of accepted love, with a pulse that ever sinks into more and more normal beat, with an ever steadier and deeper flush of the new-born life. And here, if the reader will lay down the book at the close of sonnet 18, he may interpolate the lovely lyric called " Inclusions " :

*Oh, wilt thou have my hand, Dear, to lie along
  in thine?*
*As a little stone in a running stream, it seems
  to lie and pine.*
*Now drop the poor pale hand, Dear, unfit to
  pledge with thine.*

*Oh, wilt thou have my cheek, Dear, drawn
  closer to thine own?*
*My cheek is white, my cheek is worn, by many
  a tear run down.*
*Now leave a little space, Dear, lest it should
  wet thine own.*

*Oh, must thou have my soul, Dear, commingled
  with thy soul?*
*Red grows the cheek, and warm the hand; the
  part is in the whole ·*
*Nor hands nor cheeks keep separate, when soul
  is joined to soul.*

We may pursue no further, save in the
divine words of the sonnets themselves, the
record of this noble and exquisite "marriage
of true minds." But we may be thankful
that the accredited chronicle of this episode
in life and literature, lifted far out of any
vagueness of conjecture or possibility of
misconstruction, exists for us, distinguishing,
illuminating, perfuming a great page of our

national poetry. Many of the thoughts that enrich mankind and many of the purest flowers of the imagination had their roots, if the secrets of experience were made known, in actions, in desires, which could not bear the light of day, in hot-beds smelling quite otherwise than of violet or sweetbriar. But this cycle of admirable sonnets, one of the acknowledged glories of our literature, is built patently and unquestionably on the union in stainless harmony of two of the most distinguished spirits which our century has produced.

EDMUND GOSSE.

1894.

SONNETS
FROM THE PORTUGUESE

I THOUGHT once how Theocritus had sung
  Of the sweet years, the dear and wished-for years,
Who each one in a gracious hand appears
To bear a gift for mortals, old or young:
And, as I mused it in his antique tongue,
I saw, in gradual vision through my tears,
The sweet, sad years, the melancholy years,
Those of my own life, who by turns had flung
A shadow across me.   Straightway I was 'ware,
So weeping, how a mystic Shape did move
Behind me, and drew me backward by the hair;
And a voice said in mastery, while I strove,—
"Guess now who holds thee?"—"Death," I said.
        But, there,
The silver answer rang,—"Not Death, but Love."

II.

BUT only three in all God's universe
   Have heard this word thou hast said,—Himself,
      beside
Thee speaking, and me listening! and replied
One of us . . . *that* was God, . . . and laid the curse
So darkly on my eyelids, as to amerce
My sight from seeing thee,—that if I had died,
The deathweights, placed there, would have signified
Less absolute exclusion. "Nay" is worse ˙
From God than from all others, O my friend!
Men could not part us with their worldly jars,
Nor the seas change us, nor the tempests bend;
Our hands would touch for all the mountain-bars:
And, heaven being rolled between us at the end,
We should but vow the faster for the stars.

III.

UNLIKE are we, unlike, O princely Heart!
   Unlike our uses and our destinies.
Our ministering two angels look surprise
On one another, as they strike athwart
Their wings in passing. Thou, bethink thee, art
A guest for queens to social pageantries,
With gages from a hundred brighter eyes
Than tears even can make mine, to play thy part
Of chief musician. What hast *thou* to do
With looking from the lattice-lights at me,
A poor, tired, wandering singer, singing through
The dark, and leaning up a cypress tree?
The chrism is on thine head,—on mine, the dew,—
And Death must dig the level where these agree.

IV.

THOU hast thy calling to some palace-floor,
  Most gracious singer of high poems! where
The dancers will break footing, from the care
Of watching up thy pregnant lips for more.
And dost thou lift this house's latch too poor
For hand of thine? and canst thou think and bear
To let thy music drop here unaware
In folds of golden fulness at my door?
Look up and see the casement broken in,
The bats and owlets builders in the roof!
My cricket chirps against thy mandolin.
Hush, call no echo up in further proof
Of desolation! there 's a voice within
That weeps   . as thou must sing   alone, aloof.

V.

I LIFT my heavy heart up solemnly,
 As once Electra her sepulchral urn,
And, looking in thine eyes, I overturn
The ashes at thy feet. Behold and see
What a great heap of grief lay hid in me,
And how the red wild sparkles dimly burn
Through the ashen greyness. If thy foot in scorn
Could tread them out to darkness utterly,
It might be well perhaps. But if instead
Thou wait beside me for the wind to blow
The grey dust up, . . . those laurels on thine head,
O my Belovèd, will not shield thee so,
That none of all the fires shall scorch and shred
The hair beneath. Stand further off then! go.

Go from me. Yet I feel that I shall stand
    Henceforward in thy shadow. Nevermore
Alone upon the threshold of my door
Of individual life, I shall command
The uses of my soul, nor lift my hand
Serenely in the sunshine as before,
Without the sense of that which I forebore—
Thy touch upon the palm. The widest land
Doom takes to part us, leaves thy heart in mine
With pulses that beat double. What I do
And what I dream include thee, as the wine
Must taste of its own grapes. And when I sue
God for myself, He hears that name of thine,
And sees within my eyes the tears of two.

VII.

THE face of all the world is changed, I think,
   Since first I heard the footsteps of thy soul
Move still, oh, still, beside me, as they stole
Betwixt me and the dreadful outer brink
Of obvious death, where I, who thought to sink,
Was caught up into love, and taught the whole
Of life in a new rhythm.   The cup of dole
God gave for baptism, I am fain to drink,
And praise its sweetness, Sweet, with thee anear.
The names of country, heaven, are changed away
For where thou art or shalt be, there or here;
And this . . this lute and song   loved yesterday,
(The singing angels know) are only dear
Because thy name moves right in what they say.

VIII.

WHAT can I give thee back, O liberal
    And princely giver, who hast brought the gold
And purple of thine heart, unstained, untold,
And laid them on the outside of the wall
For such as I to take or leave withal,
In unexpected largesse? am I cold,
Ungrateful, that for these most manifold
High gifts, I render nothing back at all?
Not so; not cold,—but very poor instead.
Ask God who knows. For frequent tears have run
The colours from my life, and left so dead
And pale a stuff, it were not fitly done
To give the same as pillow to thy head.
Go farther! let it serve to trample on.

C AN it be right to give what I can give?
  To let thee sit beneath the fall of tears
As salt as mine, and hear the sighing years
Re-sighing on my lips renunciative
Through those infrequent smiles which fail to live
For all thy adjurations?　O my fears,
That this can scarce be right!　We are not peers,
So to be lovers; and I own, and grieve,
That givers of such gifts as mine are, must
Be counted with the ungenerous.　Out, alas!
I will not soil thy purple with my dust,
Nor breathe my poison on thy Venice-glass,
Nor give thee any love—which were unjust.
Beloved, I only love thee! let it pass.

X.

YET, love, mere love, is beautiful indeed
    And worthy of acceptation.   Fire is bright,
Let temple burn, or flax; an equal light
Leaps in the flame from cedar-plank or weed:
And love is fire.   And when I say at need
I love thee .   mark ! . . *I love thee*—in thy sight
I stand transfigured, glorified aright,
With conscience of the new rays that proceed
Out of my face toward thine.   There 's nothing low
In love, when love the lowest: meanest creatures
Who love God, God accepts while loving so.
And what I *feel*, across the inferior features
Of what I *am*, doth flash itself, and show
How that great work of Love enhances Nature's.

A ND therefore if to love can be desert,
    I am not all unworthy. Cheeks as pale
As these you see, and trembling knees that fail
To bear the burden of a heavy heart,—
This weary minstrel-life that once was girt
To climb Aornus, and can scarce avail
To pipe now 'gainst the valley nightingale
A melancholy music,—why advert
To these things? O Belovèd, it is plain
I am not of thy worth nor for thy place!
And yet, because I love thee, I obtain
From that same love this vindicating grace,
To live on still in love, and yet in vain,—
To bless thee, yet renounce thee to thy face.

XII.

INDEED this very love which is my boast,
   And which, when rising up from breast to brow,
Doth crown me with a ruby large enow
To draw men's eyes and prove the inner cost,—
This love even, all my worth, to the uttermost,
I should not love withal, unless that thou
Hadst set me an example, shown me how,
When first thine earnest eyes with mine were crossed,
And love called love. And thus, I cannot speak
Of love even, as a good thing of my own:
Thy soul hath snatched up mine all faint and weak,
And placed it by thee on a golden throne,—
And that I love (O soul, we must be meek!)
Is by thee only, whom I love alone.

A ND wilt thou have me fashion into speech
    The love I bear thee, finding words enough,
And hold the torch out, while the winds are rough,
Between our faces, to cast light on each ?—
I drop it at thy feet. I cannot teach
My hand to hold my spirit so far off
From myself—me—that I should bring thee proof
In words, of love hid in me out of reach.
Nay, let the silence of my womanhood
Commend my woman-love to thy belief,—
Seeing that I stand unwon, however wooed,
And rend the garment of my life, in brief,
By a most dauntless, voiceless fortitude,
Lest one touch of this heart convey its grief.

XIV.

IF thou must love me, let it be for nought
   Except for love's sake only. Do not say
"I love her for her smile—her look—her way
Of speaking gently,—for a trick of thought
That falls in well with mine, and certes brought
A sense of pleasant ease on such a day"—
For these things in themselves, Belovèd, may
Be changed, or change for thee,—and love, so wrought,
May be unwrought so. Neither love me for
Thine own dear pity 's wiping my cheeks dry,—
A creature might forget to weep, who bore
Thy comfort long, and lose thy love thereby!
But love me for love's sake, that evermore
Thou mayst love on, through love's eternity.

A CCUSE me not, beseech thee, that I wear
    Too calm and sad a face in front of thine;
For we two look two ways, and cannot shine
With the same sunlight on our brow and hair.
On me thou lookest with no doubting care,
As on a bee shut in a crystalline;
Since sorrow hath shut me safe in love's divine,
And to spread wing and fly in the outer air
Were most impossible failure, if I strove
To fail so. But I look on thee—on thee—
Beholding, besides love, the end of love,
Hearing oblivion beyond memory;
As one who sits and gazes from above,
Over the rivers to the bitter sea.

XVI.

And yet, because thou overcomest so,
　　Because thou art more noble and like a king,
Thou canst prevail against my fears and fling
Thy purple round me, till my heart shall grow
Too close against thine heart henceforth to know
How it shook when alone.　Why, conquering
May prove as lordly and complete a thing
In lifting upward, as in crushing low!
And as a vanquished soldier yields his sword
To one who lifts him from the bloody earth,
Even so, Belovèd, I at last record,
Here ends my strife.　If *thou* invite me forth,
I rise above abasement at the word.
Make thy love larger to enlarge my worth.

XVII.

MY poet, thou canst touch on all the notes
    God set between His After and Before,
And strike up and strike off the general roar
Of the rushing worlds a melody that floats
In a serene air purely.   Antidotes
Of medicated music, answering for
Mankind's forlornest uses, thou canst pour
From thence into their ears.   God's will devotes
Thine to such ends, and mine to wait on thine.
How, Dearest, wilt thou have me for most use?
A hope, to sing by gladly? or a fine
Sad memory, with thy songs to interfuse?
A shade, in which to sing—of palm or pine?
A grave, on which to rest from singing?   Choose.

XVIII.

I NEVER gave a lock of hair away
  To a man, Dearest, except this to thee,
Which now upon my fingers thoughtfully,
I ring out to the full brown length and say
"Take it." My day of youth went yesterday;
My hair no longer bounds to my foot's glee,
Nor plant I it from rose or myrtle-tree,
As girls do, any more: it only may
Now shade on two pale cheeks the mark of tears,
Taught drooping from the head that hangs aside
Through sorrow's trick. I thought the funeral-shears
Would take this first, but Love is justified,—
Take it thou,—finding pure, from all those years,
The kiss my mother left here when she died.

XIX.

THE soul's Rialto hath its merchandise;
  I barter curl for curl upon that mart,
And from my poet's forehead to my heart
Receive this lock which outweighs argosies,—
As purply black, as erst to Pindar's eyes
The dim purpureal tresses gloomed athwart
The nine white Muse-brows. For this counterpart,
The bay-crown's shade, Belovèd, I surmise,
Still lingers on thy curl, it is so black!
Thus, with a fillet of smooth-kissing breath,
I tie the shadows safe from gliding back,
And lay the gift where nothing hindereth;
Here on my heart, as on thy brow, to lack
No natural heat till mine grows cold in death.

BELOVED, my Belovèd, when I think
That thou wast in the world a year ago,
What time I sat alone here in the snow
And saw no footprint, heard the silence sink
No moment at thy voice, but, link by link,
Went counting all my chains as if that so
They never could fall off at any blow
Struck by thy possible hand,—why, thus I drink
Of life's great cup of wonder! Wonderful,
Never to feel thee thrill the day or night
With personal act or speech,—nor ever cull
Some prescience of thee with the blossoms white
Thou sawest growing! Atheists are as dull,
Who cannot guess God's presence out of sight.

SAY over again, and yet once over again,
    That thou dost love me. Though the word
        repeated
Should seem "a cuckoo-song," as thou dost treat it.
Remember, never to the hill or plain,
Valley and wood, without her cuckoo-strain
Comes the fresh Spring in all her green completed.
Belovèd, I, amid the darkness greeted
By a doubtful spirit-voice, in that doubt's pain
Cry, "Speak once more—thou lovest!" Who can fear
Too many stars, though each in heaven shall roll,
Too many flowers, though each shall crown the year?
Say thou dost love me, love me, love me—toll
The silver iterance!—only minding, Dear,
To love me also in silence with thy soul.

XXII.

WHEN our two souls stand up erect and strong,
    Face to face, silent, drawing nigh and nigher,
Until the lengthening wings break into fire
At either curvèd point,—what bitter wrong
Can the earth do to us, that we should not long
Be here contented? Think. In mounting higher,
The angels would press on us and aspire
To drop some golden orb of perfect song
Into our deep, dear silence. Let us stay
Rather on earth, Belovèd,—where the unfit
Contrarious moods of men recoil away
And isolate pure spirits, and permit
A place to stand and love in for a day,
With darkness and the death-hour rounding it.

XXIII.

Is it indeed so? If I lay here dead,
   Wouldst thou miss any life in losing mine?
And would the sun for thee more coldly shine
Because of grave-damps falling round my head?
I marvelled, my Belovèd, when I read
Thy thought so in the letter. I am thine—
But . . . *so* much to thee? Can I pour thy wine
While my hands tremble? Then my soul, instead
Of dreams of death, resumes life's lower range.
Then, love me, Love! look on me—breathe on me!
As brighter ladies do not count it strange,
For love, to give up acres and degree,
I yield the grave for thy sake, and exchange
My near sweet view of Heaven, for earth with thee!

XXIV.

L ET the world's sharpness, like a clasping knife,
　　Shut in upon itself and do no harm
In this close hand of Love, now soft and warm,
And let us hear no sound of human strife
After the click of the shutting.　Life to life—
I lean upon thee, Dear, without alarm,
And feel as safe as guarded by a charm
Against the stab of worldlings, who if rife
Are weak to injure.　Very whitely still
The lilies of our lives may reassure
Their blossoms from their roots, accessible
Alone to heavenly dews that drop not fewer
Growing straight, out of man's reach, on the hill.
God only, who made us rich, can make us poor.

XXV.

A HEAVY heart, Belovèd, have I borne
    From year to year until I saw thy face,
And sorrow after sorrow took the place
Of all those natural joys as lightly worn
As the stringed pearls, each lifted in its turn
By a beating heart at dance-time. Hopes apace
Were changed to long despairs, till God's own grace
Could scarcely lift above the world forlorn
My heavy heart. Then *thou* didst bid me bring
And let it drop adown thy calmly great
Deep being! Fast it sinketh, as a thing
Which its own nature doth precipitate,
While thine doth close above it, mediating
Betwixt the stars and the unaccomplished fate.

I LIVED with visions for my company
Instead of men and women, years ago,
And found them gentle mates, nor thought to know
A sweeter music than they played to me.
But soon their trailing purple was not free
Of this world's dust, their lutes did silent grow,
And I myself grew faint and blind below
Their vanishing eyes.   Then THOU didst come—to be,
Belovèd, what they seemed.   Their shining fronts,
Their songs, their splendours (better, yet the same,
As river-water hallowed into fonts),
Met in thee, and from out thee overcame
My soul with satisfaction of all wants:
Because God's gifts put man's best dreams to shame.

XXVII.

M<small>Y</small> own Belovèd, who hast lifted me
    From this drear flat of earth where I was thrown,
And, in betwixt the languid ringlets, blown
A life-breath, till the forehead hopefully
Shines out again, as all the angels see,
Before thy saving kiss! My own, my own,
Who camest to me when the world was gone,
And I who looked for only God, found *thee!*
I find thee; I am safe, and strong, and glad.
As one who stands in dewless asphodel
Looks backward on the tedious time he had
In the upper life,—so I, with bosom-swell,
Make witness, here, between the good and bad,
That Love, as strong as Death, retrieves as well.

XXVIII.

M<small>Y</small> letters! all dead paper, mute and white !
  And yet they seem alive and quivering
Against my tremulous hands which loose the string
And let them drop down on my knee to-night.
This said,—he wished to have me in his sight
Once, as a friend : this fixed a day in spring
To come and touch my hand . . . a simple thing,
Yet I wept for it!—this, . . . the paper's light . .
Said, *Dear, I love thee;* and I sank and quailed
As if God's future thundered on my past.
This said, *I am thine*—and so its ink has paled
With lying at my heart that beat too fast.
And this . . O Love, thy words have ill availed
If, what this said, I dared repeat at last !

XXIX.

I THINK of thee!—my thoughts do twine and bud
   About thee, as wild vines, about a tree,
Put out broad leaves, and soon there 's nought to see
Except the straggling green which hides the wood.
Yet, O my palm-tree, be it understood
I will not have my thoughts instead of thee
Who art dearer, better! Rather, instantly
Renew thy presence; as a strong tree should,
Rustle thy boughs and set thy trunk all bare,
And let these bands of greenery which insphere thee
Drop heavily down,—burst, shattered, everywhere!
Because, in this deep joy to see and hear thee
And breathe within thy shadow a new air,
I do not think of thee—I am too near thee.

XXX.

I SEE thine image through my tears to-night,
  And yet to-day I saw thee smiling.   How
Refer the cause?—Belovèd, is it thou
Or I, who makes me sad?   The acolyte
Amid the chanted joy and thankful rite
May so fall flat, with pale insensate brow,
On the altar-stair.   I hear thy voice and vow,
Perplexed, uncertain, since thou art out of sight,
As he, in his swooning ears, the choir's Amen.
Belovèd, dost thou love? or did I see all
The glory as I dreamed, and fainted when
Too vehement light dilated my ideal,
For my soul's eyes?   Will that light come again,
As now these tears come—falling hot and real?

XXXI.

THOU comest! all is said without a word.
  I sit beneath thy looks, as children do
In the noon-sun, with souls that tremble through
Their happy eyelids from an unaverred
Yet prodigal inward joy. Behold, I erred
In that last doubt! and yet I cannot rue
The sin most, but the occasion—that we two
Should for a moment stand unministered
By a mutual presence. Ah, keep near and close,
Thou dovelike help! and, when my fears would rise,
With thy broad heart serenely interpose:
Brood down with thy divine sufficiencies
These thoughts which tremble when bereft of those,
Like callow birds left desert to the skies.

XXXII.

THE first time that the sun rose on thine oath
    To love me, I looked forward to the moon
To slacken all those bonds which seemed too soon
And quickly tied to make a lasting troth.
Quick-loving hearts, I thought, may quickly loathe;
And, looking on myself, I seemed not one
For such man's love!—more like an out-of-tune
Worn viol, a good singer would be wroth
To spoil his song with, and which, snatched in haste,
Is laid down at the first ill-sounding note.
I did not wrong myself so, but I placed
A wrong on *thee*.   For perfect strains may float
'Neath master-hands, from instruments defaced,—
And great souls, at one stroke, may do and doat.

Yes, call me by my pet-name! let me hear
    The name I used to run at, when a child,
From innocent play, and leave the cowslips piled,
To glance up in some face that proved me dear
With the look of its eyes. I miss the clear
Fond voices which, being drawn and reconciled
Into the music of Heaven's undefiled,
Call me no longer. Silence on the bier,
While I call God—call God!—So let thy mouth
Be heir to those who are now exanimate.
Gather the north flowers to complete the south,
And catch the early love up in the late.
Yes, call me by that name,—and I, in truth,
With the same heart, will answer and not wait.

XXXIV.

WITH the same heart, I said, I 'll answer thee
　　As those, when thou shalt call me by my name—
Lo, the vain promise! is the same, the same,
Perplexed and ruffled by life's strategy?
When called before, I told how hastily
I dropped my flowers or brake off from a game,
To run and answer with the smile that came
At play last moment, and went on with me
Through my obedience. When I answer now,
I drop a grave thought, break from solitude;
Yet still my heart goes to thee—ponder how—
Not as to a single good, but all my good!
Lay thy hand on it, best one, and allow
That no child's foot could run fast as this blood.

IF I leave all for thee, wilt thou exchange
    And be all to me?   Shall I never miss
Home-talk and blessing and the common kiss
That comes to each in turn, nor count it strange,
When I look up, to drop on a new range
Of walls and floors, another home than this?
Nay, wilt thou fill that place by me which is
Filled by dead eyes too tender to know change?
That 's hardest.   If to conquer love, has tried,
To conquer grief, tries more, as all things prove;
For grief indeed is love and grief beside.
Alas, I have grieved so I am hard to love.
Yet love me—wilt thou?   Open thine heart wide,
And fold within the wet wings of thy dove.

WHEN we met first and loved, I did not build
    Upon the event with marble.   Could it mean
To last, a love set pendulous between
Sorrow and sorrow?   Nay, I rather thrilled,
Distrusting every light that seemed to gild
The onward path, and feared to overlean
A finger even.   And, though I have grown serene
And strong since then, I think that God has willed
A still renewable fear . . . O love, O troth .
Lest these enclaspèd hands should never hold,
This mutual kiss drop down between us both
As an unowned thing, once the lips being cold.
And Love, be false! if *he*, to keep one oath,
Must lose one joy, by his life's star foretold.

PARDON, oh, pardon, that my soul should make,
  Of all that strong divineness which I know
For thine and thee, an image only so
Formed of the sand, and fit to shift and break.
It is that distant years which did not take
Thy sovranty, recoiling with a blow,
Have forced my swimming brain to undergo
Their doubt and dread, and blindly to forsake
Thy purity of likeness and distort
Thy worthiest love to a worthless counterfeit:
As if a shipwrecked Pagan, safe in port,
His guardian sea-god to commemorate,
Should set a sculptured porpoise, gills a-snort
And vibrant tail, within the temple-gate.

XXXVIII.

FIRST time he kissed me, he but only kissed
    The fingers of this hand wherewith I write;
And ever since, it grew more clean and white,
Slow to world-greetings, quick with its "Oh, list,"
When the angels speak. A ring of amethyst
I could not wear here, plainer to my sight,
Than that first kiss. The second passed in height
The first, and sought the forehead, and half missed,
Half falling on the hair. O beyond meed!
That was the chrism of love, which love's own crown,
With sanctifying sweetness, did precede.
The third upon my lips was folded down
In perfect, purple state; since when, indeed,
I have been proud and said, "My love, my own."

BECAUSE thou hast the power and own'st the grace
    To look through and behind this mask of me
(Against which years have beat thus blanchingly
With their rains), and behold my soul's true face,
The dim and weary witness of life's race,—
Because thou hast the faith and love to see,
Through that same soul's distracting lethargy,
The patient angel waiting for a place
In the new Heavens,—because nor sin nor woe,
Nor God's infliction, nor death's neighbourhood,
Nor all which others viewing, turn to go,
Nor all which makes me tired of all, self-viewed,—
Nothing repels thee,   Dearest, teach me so
To pour out gratitude, as thou dost, good!

OH, yes! they love through all this world of ours!
 I will not gainsay love, called love forsooth.
I have heard love talked in my early youth,
And since, not so long back but that the flowers
Then gathered, smell still. Mussulmans and Giaours
Throw kerchiefs at a smile, and have no ruth
For any weeping. Polypheme's white tooth
Slips on the nut if, after frequent showers,
The shell is over-smooth,—and not so much
Will turn the thing called love, aside to hate
Or else to oblivion. But thou art not such
A lover, my Belovèd! thou canst wait
Through sorrow and sickness, to bring souls to touch,
And think it soon when others cry "Too late."

I THANK all who have loved me in their hearts,
   With thanks and love from mine.   Deep thanks
       to all
Who paused a little near the prison-wall
To hear my music in its louder parts
Ere they went onward, each one to the mart's
Or temple's occupation, beyond call.
But thou, who, in my voice's sink and fall
When the sob took it, thy divinest Art's
Own instrument didst drop down at thy foot
To hearken what I said between my tears,
Instruct me how to thank thee! Oh, to shoot
My soul's full meaning into future years,
That *they* should lend it utterance, and salute
Love that endures, from Life that disappears!

"My *future will not copy fair my past*"—
 I wrote that once; and thinking at my side
My ministering life-angel justified
The word by his appealing look upcast
To the white throne of God, I turned at last,
And there, instead, saw thee, not unallied
To angels in thy soul! Then I, long tried
By natural ills, received the comfort fast,
While budding, at thy sight, my pilgrim's staff
Gave out green leaves with morning dews impearled.
I seek no copy now of life's first half:
Leave here the pages with long musing curled,
And write me new my future's epigraph,
New angel mine, unhoped for in the world!

XLIII.

How do I love thee? Let me count the ways.
 I love thee to the depth and breadth and height
My soul can reach, when feeling out of sight
For the ends of Being and ideal Grace.
I love thee to the level of everyday's
Most quiet need, by sun and candlelight.
I love thee freely, as men strive for Right;
I love thee purely, as they turn from Praise.
I love thee with the passion put to use
In my old griefs, and with my childhood's faith.
I love thee with a love I seemed to lose
With my lost saints,—I love thee with the breath,
Smiles, tears, of all my life!—and, if God choose,
I shall but love thee better after death.

Beloved, thou hast brought me many flowers
  Plucked in the garden, all the summer through
And winter, and it seemed as if they grew
In this close room, nor missed the sun and showers.
So, in the like name of that love of ours,
Take back these thoughts which here unfolded too,
And which on warm and cold days I withdrew
From my heart's ground. Indeed, those beds and
    bowers
Be overgrown with bitter weeds and rue,
And wait thy weeding; yet here 's eglantine,
Here 's ivy!—take them, as I used to do
Thy flowers, and keep them where they shall not pine.
Instruct thine eyes to keep their colours true,
And tell thy soul their roots are left in mine.

Made in the USA
Coppell, TX
07 November 2021